Denali
Walks

by Kris Capps

Alaska Natural History Association
Anchorage, Alaska

Alaska Natural History Association thanks
Denali National Park and Preserve for their assistance in developing and
reviewing this publication. The Alaska Natural History Association
works in partnership with the National Park Service to further public
education and appreciation for national parks in Alaska.
The publication of books, among other activities, support
and complement the National Park Service mission.

AUTHOR: Kris Capps
EDITOR: Martha Bistrow
DESIGN AND MAPS: Chris Byrd
PROJECT COORDINATOR: Lisa Oakley
NATIONAL PARK SERVICE COORDINATOR: Marisa James
PHOTOGRAPHY: © Fred Hirschmann: 19, 35, 43
© Ron Niebrugge/wildnatureimages.com: Cover, 1, 11, 13, 16, 27, 37
Gerry Reynolds: 8
ILLUSTRATIONS: Denise Ekstrand: 7, 25

Published by the Alaska Natural History Association
in cooperation with the National Park Service.

Alaska
Natural History
ASSOCIATION

Alaska Natural History Association
750 West Second Avenue, Suite 100
Anchorage, Alaska 99501

www.alaskanha.org

Alaska Natural History Association is a nonprofit publisher of
books and other materials about Alaska's public lands. For more
information or to become a supporting member: www.alaskanha.org

ISBN-10: 9-930931-83-1
ISBN-13: 978-0-930931-83-4

Printed in China on recycled paper using soy based inks.

Introduction

The best way to experience the trails of Denali National Park and Preserve is to immerse yourself in the wildness of this place. Just a few steps lead into the taiga forest, filled with shrubs, trees, and wildlife, or the vast landscape of the open tundra. Do more than focus on the trail ahead. Feel the wind caress your face. Hear the breeze rustle through the trees and sweep over ridges. Smell wildflowers, the scent of a summer shower, or the faint, spicy aroma of Labrador tea beneath your feet. Listen for the chatter of red squirrels or the gurgling of a mountain stream. Each trail offers a one-of-a-kind experience in what you can smell and hear, as well as what you can see. If you take a moment to engage all of those senses, you will feel the wilderness. Immerse yourself and you'll truly experience Denali National Park and Preserve.

Trails listed in this book lead through taiga forest and over open tundra.

No one is quite sure where the word "taiga" comes from. For many years, people believed it was a Finnish word that means "Land of Little Sticks." It's not hard to see why that story persisted. Black spruce trees often look like little sticks.

This sub-arctic forest also includes robust white spruce, as well as aspen, paper birch, and balsam poplar. Dwarf birch and willow thrive near knee-level and a rich carpet of mosses, lichens, fungi, wildflowers, and ankle-high shrubs live on the forest floor.

Tundra is the land above treeline, which occurs at about 3,000 feet in Denali National Park and Preserve. Here, plant life hugs the ground closely. There are two types of tundra: moist and dry. Moist tundra features waist-high thickets of willow and dwarf birch near patches of spruce. Blueberries grow here. Foot travel may be difficult because of hummocks—lumpy clusters of grasses and sedges surrounded by lichens, mosses, and horsetails—and standing water.

Dry or alpine tundra covers mountain slopes. Soil is thin and the growing season is short. These tundra plants survive wind, bitter cold, snow, ice, and trampling by hikers.

Most trails are located along the road corridor. They were constructed to protect fragile vegetation in areas popular with park visitors. Although this land may seem vast, at this latitude, it is also fragile. When plants underfoot are continually crushed, they take years to recover, so please stay on the trail.

Evidence of this can still be seen in parts of the park's entrance area. Places where many people detour off of the trail, squashing fragile plants underfoot, are called "social trails." These trails are obvious, sometimes running helter-skelter through the woods.

By providing easily accessible trails to taiga and tundra and continuing to re-vegetate trampled areas, the National Park Service hopes to return those "social trails" to their natural state so future visitors can experience the park in as healthy, beautiful and wild a state as the very first visitors.

When hiking in the backcountry, however, feel free to strike out and find a route of your own. The footsteps of one person leave no trace, but repeated travel on the same path may leave a permanent scar. Avoid walking single file and spread out when hiking together.

The best way to preserve wilderness is to make sure the next hiker who follows you never knows you were here. Leave no trace of your visit! Here are some tips to help visitors keep Denali wild.

Stay on the trail. Walking off the trail damages fragile vegetation, begins soil erosion, and causes unsightly scars on the landscape.

Take only photographs. Please leave rocks, flowers, feathers, bark, and other treasures in their natural state so others may enjoy them. These items serve as important resources for plants and animals. Flowers are a source of food, feathers may be used for nests, and bone may be chewed by rodents for minerals. Rocks may provide a protective niche for a seed to grow.

 Leave only footprints. Be especially careful to pack out all trash, including cigarette butts, toilet paper, and food scraps. And if possible, don't even leave footprints!

Do not feed wildlife. Do not leave food unattended. Please resist the urge to offer handouts to aggressive birds and squirrels.

Keep your distance from wildlife. Do not approach animals closely or pursue them. If they alter their behavior because of your presence, move farther away.

Leave your dog behind. Pets are not allowed on any trails or in the wilderness of Denali National Park and Preserve.

Weather

Although clouds and rain generally mark summer weather at Denali National Park and Preserve, day hikers must prepare for sudden changes throughout the day. Because of high peaks in the Alaska Range, weather can change quickly and dramatically. Denali National Park gets only 15 inches of rain a year, but most of that falls during summer months in light, occasional showers. Snowfall is possible throughout the summer, as are blistering, 80-degree days. Prepare for anything, because you will probably experience it all. And don't forget your head net and insect repellent. Mosquitoes can be fierce here, regardless of the weather.

What to Bring

- Water
- Snacks
- Binoculars
- Warm hat and gloves
- Sunscreen and sunglasses
- Insect repellant
- Layered clothing
- Sturdy shoes
- Rain- and wind-proof outerwear

Wildlife

Opportunities for viewing wildlife exist on every trail. Out on the tundra, no trees obscure the view. Patience and persistence can lead to sightings of many inhabitants of Denali National Park and Preserve.

Respect the animals and their homes. Don't go closer than the minimum distance restrictions shown below. Any distance that alters the behavior of an animal is too close. Resist the temptation to approach animals to take photographs or to see them more easily. Carry binoculars or use a telephoto lens. Enjoy Denali's wild animals from a distance.

Here are some of the animals you may encounter and where to look for them:

- **Pika** – rock piles on mountainsides

- **Marmot** – rock piles on mountain sides

- **Snowshoe hare** – taiga forest

- **Beaver** – streams and ponds

- **Porcupine** – taiga forest

- **Red fox, coyote, wolf** – taiga or tundra

- **Grizzly bear** – tundra and occasionally taiga

- **Muskrat** – ponds

- **Lynx** – taiga forest (Sightings of this cat are very rare.)

- **Moose** – taiga or tundra

- **Caribou** – tundra

- **Dall sheep** – alpine tundra mountainsides

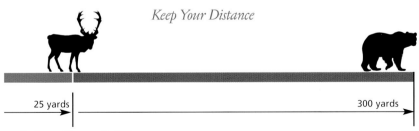

Keep Your Distance

25 yards

300 yards

Caribou, Moose, Dall Sheep,
Lynx, Wolf, Fox, Coyote,
Bird Nests, Baby Birds, Animal Dens

Bear

Trails

Entrance Area

There's more than one way to enter Denali National Park and Preserve. You can drive a motor vehicle or you can travel by foot. Walking may not get you to the Wilderness Access Center as quickly, but in reality, walking gets you into the wilderness itself sooner.

From the entrance area, there are two paths you can follow to the Wilderness Access Center or the Denali Visitor Center. Both go through the taiga forest.

Front Country Trails

Several trails begin within the first few miles of the park entrance. All can be reached from the Denali Visitor Center. Depending on the trail, these hikes can fill a morning, a full day, an hour, or less. You can choose anything from an easy stroll through the forest to a hike up to the Healy overlook for outstanding views.

Bike Path

Trailhead: Nenana Canyon developed area and Denali Visitor Center. Trail can also be accessed at many road crossings in between these two points.

Distance/Time: 1.7 miles/2.7 kilometers one way between south end of Nenana River pedestrian bridge and Denali Visitor Center, 45 minutes.

Terrain: 120-inch-wide, part paved and part well-compacted gravel surface, 150 foot/50 meter elevation change with maximum grade of 5 percent, the slope of a wheelchair ramp.

Difficulty: Easy, wheelchair accessible.

This trail is a continuation of a bike path that begins outside of the park at the south end of the developed area, north of the park entrance. It crosses the Nenana River on a pedestrian bridge before entering the park. From here this wide, paved path runs from the south end of the footbridge to the beginning of the Park Road. A line of trees shields hikers or bicyclists from heavy traffic on the George Parks Highway. Just 200 yards from the bridge is a small turnout and the Denali National Park sign, a popular photo stop for visitors. Further along, the pavement ends and the path continues on a graveled surface, running from the park entrance to the new Denali Visitor Center. This route parallels the park road and winds through the taiga forest. It emerges across from Riley Creek Campground and Mercantile where it then follows the road to the Wilderness Access Center. There the trail veers into the taiga forest until it reaches the cluster of buildings that includes the Alaska Railroad Depot and finally, the Denali Visitor Center.

Although you are in the heart of the busy entrance area, this quick foray into the taiga forest provides a taste of wilderness.

You may see spruce cone pieces heaped in small piles along the trail. These are made by squirrels,

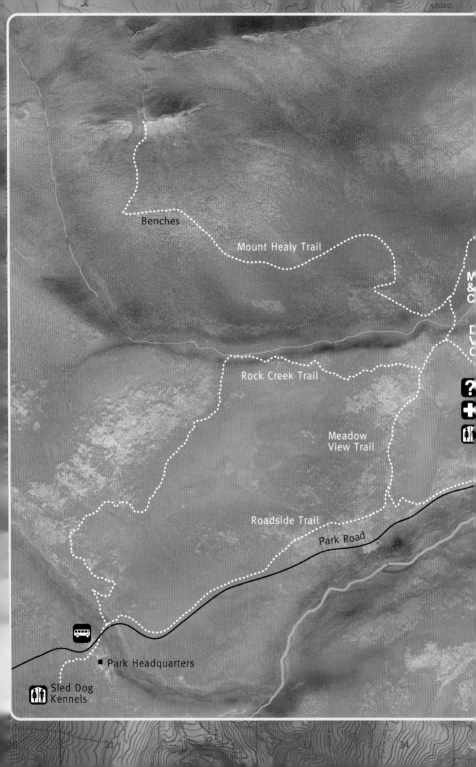

Benches

Mount Healy Trail

M
&
C

D
V
C

Rock Creek Trail

Meadow
View Trail

Roadside Trail

Park Road

Park Headquarters

Sled Dog
Kennels

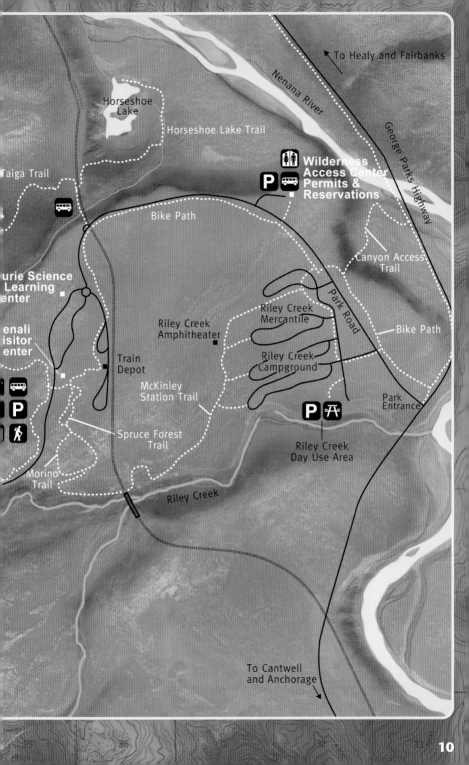

the most visible residents of the forest. There are only two species of squirrels in Denali National Park that live in the taiga forest—the northern flying squirrel and the red squirrel. Flying squirrels are rarely spotted, but the red squirrel makes itself easily known by incessant chattering. Both populations ebb and flow with the production of their primary food source: white spruce cones. The white spruce cone production goes from prolific to scarce on a five- to seven-year cycle.

Once you veer away from the road, a wide swath of trees insulates you from traffic noise and you can listen for the sounds of the forest. Straight ahead, enjoy a view of Mount Healy.

Canyon Access Trail

Trailhead: Joins with the bike path just south of the Nenana River pedestrian bridge and with the Bike Path again across the Park Road from the Riley Creek Campground and Mercantile.

Distance/Time: 0.4 miles/0.7 kilometers one way, allow 20 to 30 minutes.

Terrain: 30-inch-wide gravel surface, mostly flat with one steep section, 80 foot/25 meter elevation change, maximum grade 8 percent.

Difficulty: Easy to moderate.

If you're entering the park on foot, this will be your first chance to experience the wildness of Denali National Park and Preserve away from the road system. The trail takes off to the west, just south of the Nenana River Bridge, and leads through the taiga forest. It's surprising how close you can be to civilization, yet still be removed from it. Traffic sounds from the George Parks Highway linger in the background, but they soon fade away, replaced by the roar of the nearby Nenana River.

This 30-inch-wide gravel path is easy to follow through white and black spruce forest. Follow the rock-lined path up and around a boggy area filled with black spruce. As you walk uphill, white spruce trees outnumber other species. The forest is thin enough that you'll see hotels through the trees, to the north, and gravel cliffs that line the Nenana River to the west.

The Canyon Accesss Trail connects to the Bike Trail, just before it crosses the park road, across from the entrance to the Riley Creek Mercantile.

Horseshoe Lake Trail

Trailhead: At mile 0.9 on the Park Road, follow the trail north that parallels train tracks for 200 yards and turn right, crossing the tracks, at the trail junction.

Distance/Time: 1.5 miles/2.2 kilometers roundtrip, allow 1.5 hours.

Terrain: 60-inch-wide gravel and dirt trail, mostly flat with one long, steep section and some short, steep hills, 250 foot/83 meter elevation change; steepest grade is more than 20 percent.

Difficulty: Easy to moderately strenuous.

Easily accessible and scenic, the Horseshoe Lake Trail remains one of the park's most popular day hikes. The trail begins at Mile 0.9 of the park road, near the railroad crossing, and leads up a dirt embankment and into the heart of the taiga forest. Dwarf shrubs and mosses cover the forest floor and spruce, aspen, willow, balsam poplar, and paper birch trees line the trail.

Stop at the overlook part way down the trail and you'll see Horseshoe Lake, a classic example of an oxbow lake. Once a channel of the nearby Nenana River, the stream eventually became cut off from the rest of the river and isolated.

Beavers call this lake home now. These busy creatures built a dam at the north end of the lake and a lodge on the peninsula. Both are vital to the animal's survival. Do not stand on either of these structures. The sturdy lodge is made of mud and sticks. It includes an underwater tunnel, which allows beavers to swim beneath the winter ice and collect food from an underwater cache. Inside, the lodge opens into a room above water level where beaver adults and kits reside.

In addition to beaver-chewed trees near the lake, there are many other signs of wildlife along this trail. Gnawed patches in the bark of spruce trees show that porcupines have been at work, too.

Spruce grouse survive on spruce needles throughout the winter. Red squirrels are active residents of this forest, busy collecting spruce cones and creating large "middens"—piles of gnawed spruce cones pieces. In the heart of the forest, these middens can be several yards wide and several feet deep. Squirrels can usually be heard before they are seen. Of all the creatures in this part of the park, they commonly represent the sound of the taiga forest.

The lake itself offers habitat for many creatures. Moose occasionally linger here browsing willows or, belly-deep in the lake, munching on underwater plants. Muskrats and waterfowl can also be seen here.

Many obvious social trails take off from the Horseshoe Lake Trail. Please stay on the main trail. Using those social trails causes damage to vegetation that can take many years to regenerate. Plans to renovate the Horseshoe Lake Trail and restore those trampled areas around the trail will strengthen a sense of wilderness for visitors.

Trailhead: One end is at the Denali Visitor Center. The other connects with the Bike Path near the Riley Creek Campground and Mercantile.

Distance/Time: 1.0 mile/1.6 kilometers one way, allow 60 minutes.

Terrain: 48- to 60-inch wide well-compacted gravel surface, 100 foot/30 meter elevation change, maximum grade 5 percent.

Difficulty: Moderate, ADA Accessible.

Hidden among the underbrush of the taiga forest near the Denali Visitor Center are the remnants of Denali National Park's early days. This trail provides a look at the past, when only a handful of visitors made their way to this remote national park.

This is not a loop trail. If you start at the Denali Visitor Center, you'll end at the Riley Creek Mercantile. Take a free shuttle bus back to your starting point, walk the Roadside Trail to complete a loop, or retrace your steps. Along the way, you'll get a feel for the small pioneer community that once depended upon the railroad for visitors and supplies. This early settlement was called McKinley Station and included accommodations run by Maurice

Morino, a fox farm, and some small trapper cabins.

The trail back in time begins directly in front of the Denali Visitor Center. You're on the right path if, in short order, you cross a small foot bridge. The trail turns into an old roadbed that leads to the site of Morino's second roadhouse.

This is also the location of the former walk-in, tent-only Morino Campground, which closed years ago.

Morino's second or "new" roadhouse was constructed over-looking the Alaska Railroad tracks and trestle bridge, near the newly constructed railroad that arrived in the Denali area in the early

1920s. The two-story, log road-house, which operated from 1921 until the late 1930s, was designed to look like an Italian villa of his homeland. All that remains today is a single line of tall balsam poplar trees, all in a row, which he planted along the front of the roadhouse. A large open area marks the site of Morino's greenhouse. A large hole in the ground is what remains of a cellar that housed Morino's generator, which produced electricity for the roadhouse.

The trail continues along the edge of the bluff, above the creek and the confluence of Hines Creek and Riley Creek. The first Park Headquarters was located just upstream of the confluence until 1925, when the first superintendent moved headquarters about a mile and a half away to its present location.

The trail continues under the current railroad trestle. A timber frame protects unsuspecting hikers from falling rocks. This is an active railroad line. **Do not climb onto the trestle.**

The trail wanders along a hillside, passing near and below the end of the park airstrip. Further down the trail is the site of Morino's original roadhouse which operated from 1914-1917. When the railroad came to the area in 1921, Morino abandoned this older site and built the new roadhouse. Several other buildings stood nearby, but very little remains from this era. The trail continues toward Riley Creek Campground, passing by vestiges of an old fox farm once run by a man named Duke Stubbs. All that remains of this operation is chicken wire fence, buried among leaves and brush on the forest floor for more than eighty years.

Eventually, the trail passes to the left of Riley Creek Campground and to the right of the Riley Creek Campground Amphitheater before leading to the Riley Creek Mercantile and along the park road to the Wilderness Access Center.

Cultural Preservation

It is against the law to remove, excavate, or damage any historic item found along the trails at Denali National Park and Preserve. That even includes rusty tin cans. Experts who study these areas can determine much about history by noting where specific artifacts are found. Once an item is removed, what can be learned from that artifact is also removed. Accurate historical knowledge comes from the context in which the historical item is discovered.

Taiga Trail

Trailhead: Denali Visitor Center or the trailhead at mile 0.9 on the Park Road (at the railroad tracks).

Distance/Time: 1.3 mile/2 kilometer connector trail, 45-60 minutes one way.

Terrain: 24- to 36-inch-wide gravel and dirt path with narrow, open drainage ditches to step across, roots and rocks. 75 foot/23 meter elevation change, maximum grade 15 percent for short sections.

Difficulty: Easy to moderate.

The Taiga Trail makes it easy to hike a complete loop through the spruce forest. The trailhead is easily reached via a short walk from the Denali Visitor Center, along the Roadside Trail, to Mile 0.9 of the Park Road. Follow the path north along the railroad tracks to the trail junction. To the right, on the other side of the tracks, is the Horseshoe Lake Trail. Turn to the left for the Taiga Trail. A gradual uphill path offers an invigorating walk through the taiga forest into big timber and away from the hustle and bustle of the entrance area. The trail connects to the Mount Healy Trail and the Rock Creek Trail.

As you hike, notice the lacy horsetail along the edge of the path. This plant has been around since the age of the dinosaurs. Also called "scouring rush," this plant's stems contain silica, which makes horsetail a great tool for scrubbing pots and pans when camping—though not when camping in a national park!

Roadside Trail

Trailhead: Denali Visitor Center or park headquarters at mile 3.2 on Park Road.

Distance/Time: 1.8 miles/3 kilometers, 45 minutes to 1 hour one way.

Terrain: 36- to 48-inch-wide well-compacted gravel surface, mostly steady but gradual hill with one-half mile of moderately steep grades, 350-foot/107 meter elevation change, maximum grade 15 percent.

Difficulty: Moderately strenuous.

If you're heading to the Park Headquarters area from the Denali Visitor Center, just about one mile away, try walking on this trail instead of on the Park Road. Wide and friendly, the Roadside Trail parallels the Park Road for most of its length, except for one-half mile when it moves away from the road and switches back up a slope. This is also an easy downhill hike back to the Denali Visitor Center after watching the sled dog demonstration in the headquarters area.

Throughout, a buffer of aspen, paper birch, and spruce trees shields you from the stream of motor vehicles on the Park Road. There are a couple of benches along the way if you need to rest. If you are walking from the Denali Visitor Center, the trail crosses a service road just east of the Rock Creek Bridge at Mile 3.0, joins the Rock Creek Trail, crosses a footbridge and the Park Road and ends at the Park Headquarters Parking Lot. Watch for gray jays, chickadees and other resident birds along this wooded trail.

Mount Healy Overlook Trail

Trailhead: Take Taiga Trail for 0.3 miles then look for Mount Healy Trailhead.

Distance/Time: 4.4 miles/7.1 kilometers roundtrip, allow 3-4 hours.

Terrain: Varies from 16 inches to 60-inch-wide loose soil surface with rocks and roots. First mile is moderately steep; remaining 1.4 miles very steep. 1,700-foot/518 meter elevation change, grades exceeding 25 percent.

Difficulty: Strenuous.

Mount Healy Trail offers an opportunity to experience most of the ecosystems represented at Denali National Park. This strenuous hike is the quickest way to reach alpine tundra in the front country. You'll begin in the taiga forest, pass over a stream, and through a thicket of alder bushes. Alders have small cones and broad leaves with serrated edges. These are pioneer plants that invade open areas soon after a disturbance such as trail or road building.

The trail winds through taiga, and a boggy area with some black spruce trees. Black spruce forests are often underlain with frozen soil called permafrost. The bog forms because the top layer of the ground thaws in the summer and the water has nowhere to drain.

Enjoy the spectacular view at the end of the first mile. Mount Fellows rises to the east and the Alaska Range fills the southern horizon. From here, the trail zig-zags through what was once a ski area on the slopes of Mount Healy, constructed as an off-duty recreational site for troops during World War II.

Continuing to the Overlook, the trail climbs about 1,300 feet in elevation. The trail ascends straight up the alder slope before turning left. You'll pass through an area filled with spruce and paper birch trees, then turn right again. Stop at a large boulder to catch your breath.

The trail wanders behind and on top of a 12-foot-high rock and offers an expansive view. To the southeast lies the broad valley of the Nenana River. The U-shaped valley of Riley Creek lies directly south, and erratics dot the ridge to the southwest. Erratics are large boulders carried long distances by advancing glaciers, and then dropped onto the landscape when the glaciers melted or receded. Mount Healy, part of Alaska's Outer Range, escaped the onset of glaciers 10,000 years ago. Its valleys are V-shaped and steep, carved by water, not ice.

The trail moves next through thickets and clearings. Please resist the urge to take shortcuts between switchbacks. Shortcuts lead to trampling of vegetation and soil erosion.

Soon, you'll emerge into open alpine country and begin to enjoy broad views of the surrounding landscape. There are no bushes, no trees. A thin mat of vegetation two to three inches thick covers the rocky soil. Here, plants hug the ground. This dry tundra provides grass and mountain avens for grazing Dall sheep and plenty of territory for arctic ground squirrels. Look skyward and maybe you'll see a golden eagle soaring overhead, scanning the tundra below, hunting for those ground squirrels.

The trail continues through the tundra and finally emerges onto the rocky shoulder of Healy Ridge, called the Healy Overlook. The actual summit of Mount Healy is far beyond.

The reward for the steep climb: spectacular views of the Nenana River Valley, Healy Ridge, and other peaks of the Alaska Range. On clear days, you may even be able to see Mount McKinley, 80 miles away.

Rock Creek Trail

Trailhead: Denali Visitor Center or take Taiga Trail from trailhead at mile 0.9 on park road to junction with Rock Creek Trail.

Distance/Time: 2.3 miles/3.7 kilometers one way, allow 2 hours.

Terrain: Nearly 30-inch-wide well-compacted gravel surface. One long steep hill and then moderate ups and downs. 400 foot/115 meter elevation change, grades up to 15 percent.

Difficulty: Moderately strenuous.

Rock Creek Trail takes you away from the noise and bustle of the entrance area, deep into the taiga forest. The beginning of the Rock Creek Trail is quite steep for the first half-mile. Then, it becomes a gentler uphill climb.

The trail winds through white spruce and aspen forest. White spruce is the predominant tree of the taiga forest, though it is the humble aspen that provides a vital food source for snowshoe hare and moose, both of which eat its bark. Take a careful look at the trunks of some of the trees and you will be able to discern who was dining. Hares make clean cuts with their sharp incisors when they munch away; moose make a jagged, ripping tear.

The floor of the taiga forest is covered with plants like Labrador tea, lowbush cranberry, and others. Some of these plants stay green year-round. Even in the middle of winter, enough light filters through the surrounding trees and the snowpack to allow photosynthesis. Summer's ever-present fireweed is easily spotted, especially as it begins opening fuchsia-colored blossoms. In the fall, plump blueberries and crowberries weigh down their respective bushes.

The understory also provides food and shelter for the small creatures of the taiga. Voles, shrews, and mice, the warm-blooded foundation of the ecosystem, eat all of those little plants and seeds on the ground.

When winter sets in, they move under the snow, using the insulation for warmth, digging a labyrinth of tunnels through the drifts. Generally solitary during the summer, red-backed voles join forces during the winter and burrow together, taking advantage of body heat from the whole colony. Like ground squirrels on the tundra, these tiny creatures live at the bottom of the forest food chain. That's why this trail also provides excellent opportunities to spot predators like goshawks and great horned owls.

At about mid-point, the forest opens to allow a sweeping view of the Yanert Valley and Mount Fellows. There's a bench here, so sit and enjoy the view. The sounds of civilization begin to die away and are replaced by the chirps of birds and rustling of leaves on trees. Gray jays hop from branch to branch following your progress. The gray jay is a year-round resident of the taiga forest, always interested in checking out human visitors.

At the end of the trail, the path drops steeply before crossing a service road and ending at the Roadside Trail. Turn right to go to Park Headquarters or left to follow the Roadside Trail back to the Denali Visitor Center for a long afternoon loop hike.

Meadow View Trail

Trailhead: This trail connects the Rock Creek Trail and the Roadside Trail.

Distance/Time: 0.25 miles/0.4 kilometers one way, allow 20 minutes.

Terrain: 18- to 24-inch wide, well-compacted gravel surface, excellent views, some steep sections.

Difficulty: Easy.

This short and narrow trail is a link between the Roadside and the Rock Creek Trails making your journey through the taiga forest into a pleasant loop.

If you are on the Rock Creek Trail, you'll hike up a steep hill to the top of a large bench. The Meadow View Trail skirts the edge of the bench for about one-third of a mile. Hikers emerge at some knolls that offer fantastic views of the Triple Lakes Ridge, the Yanert Valley, and a large meadow a couple hundred feet below. The meadow is being formed by vegetation reclaiming an old pond. Best of all, development is largely hidden from view and only the wilderness can be seen.

Along the trail, when trees thin and you catch glimpses of distant peaks in the Alaska Range, you"ll gain some perspective on the immensity of Mount McKinley, just 80 miles down the road. Most of the peaks in sight are 5,000 to 6,000 feet tall. They look huge. Although not visible from this trail, Mount McKinley, the tallest mountain in North America, rises 20,320 feet; it dwarfs these massive peaks.

Short Loops From the Visitor Center

These short loop trails are good for stretching your legs and enjoying the taiga forest, or walking off your lunch. They are short, flat, and informative. Interpretive signs on these trails will enrich your experience.

Morino Trail

Trailhead: Follow the McKinley Station Trail from the Denali Visitor Center and watch for the Morino Trail on your right. The trail loops around and connects with the McKinley Station Trail again 0.1 miles further down the trail.

Distance/Time: 0.4 miles/0.6 kilometers roundtrip from Denali Visitor Center, allow 30 minutes.

Terrain: 48-inch-wide, well-compacted gravel surface. Flat ground, no elevation change, spruce forest.

Difficulty: Easy, handicapped accessible.

This trail winds through the former homestead of Maurice Morino, who operated a road-house here in the 1920s and '30s. He homesteaded sometime between 1910 and 1920, establishing a roadhouse business near the present Riley Creek Campground. When the railroad came to Denali, he abandoned the original site and built a new roadhouse adjacent to the railroad and the new McKinley Park Station depot. He built his two-story, log roadhouse to resemble the Italian villas of his homeland. Morino catered primarily to transient workers, trappers, etc. rather than tourists who mostly stayed at Savage River Camp starting in 1923. He died in 1937. The Morino Roadhouse fell into disuse after the completion of the new, modern McKinley Park Hotel in 1939. On May 31, 1950, a traveler dropped a cigarette causing a fire that burned the old roadhouse to the ground. But remnants of that busy time are still evident today. A single line of large balsam poplar trees stands all in a row, marking the front of the former roadhouse. Morino planted those trees.

For many years, the National Park Service operated this area as a walk-in, tent-only campground called Morino Campground.

Spruce Forest Trail

Trailhead: Look for signs at the trailhead behind the Denali Visitor Center. The Spruce Forest Trail loops back around and intersects the McKinley Station Trail 0.1 miles from the Denali Visitor Center.

Distance/Time: 0.25 miles/0.4 kilometers roundtrip from Denali Visitor Center, allow 15 minutes.

Terrain: 72-inch-wide well-compacted gravel surface. Flat ground, no elevation change, spruce forest.

Difficulty: Easy, handicapped accessible.

Wide, flat and level, this trail provides an easy, short loop through the spruce forest. Visitors in wheelchairs and visitors pushing baby strollers will find easy passage on this handicap accessible trail. Small children can scurry straight down the path and back again without struggling with any hills or steep grades.

The entire loop takes only about fifteen minutes to complete. For a longer outing, hook up with the Morino Trail and double your time in the forest. Watch for red squirrels scurrying from tree to tree and gray jays following your progress as you walk. There are often tiny black-capped chick-adees feeding on seeds in the treetops. This is a mature spruce forest.

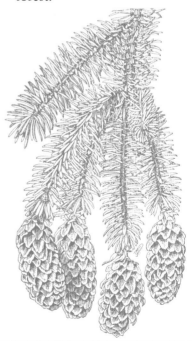

Savage River Trails

Although private vehicles may drive the 15 miles to Savage River, parking is limited, so the best way to access these trails is to take the free Savage Shuttle Bus. Trails in this section of the park offer expansive vistas with miles and miles of tundra.

One option is to hop off the bus before you reach the Savage River itself and strike out on a river bed, particularly on the north side of the road. These wide gravel bars, highways for many animals, lead directly to the high country of the Outer Alaska Range.

Whether hiking here, or along the Savage River valley, look for spruce grouse in the trees and willow ptarmigan on the ground. In winter, ptarmigan turn white, not just for camouflage but also for warmth. The lack of pigment in their feathers (as in the fur of other arctic creatures) means more room for trapped air, and thus more insulation against the cold.

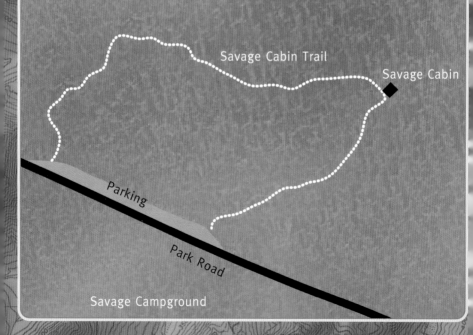

Savage Cabin Trail

Savage Cabin

Parking

Park Road

Savage Campground

Savage Cabin Interpretive Trail

Trailhead: Across from the Savage River Campground, mile 13 of the Park Road.

Distance/Time: 0.3 miles/0.5 kilometers one way, allow 20 minutes.

Terrain: Relatively flat, gravel path.

Difficulty: Easy.

This trail leads to a piece of Denali history, one of fifteen historic cabins at Denali National Park and Preserve. Most of these cabins were built between 1924 and 1935 during construction of the park road. Some were built to provide shelter for park rangers on winter patrols. This cabin, along with cabins at Sanctuary, Igloo, East Fork and Toklat, were all built as cookhouses by the Alaska Road Commission at major road construction camps.

This particular cabin used to be part of two cabins built facing each other, connected by a common roof. Originally, it sat about one mile southwest of its present location, where it served as both a cookhouse for road workers in the summer and a shelter for park rangers on patrol during the winter. In 1940, the park separated the two cabins and moved one half of it to this location. Employees reassembled the right side and turned the left side into firewood. Today, this cabin is used in the summer by the park concessionaire giving living history presentations to visitors. Actors play the role of figures from Denali's past and tell stories about history of the national park. During the winter, the cabin is still used by rangers patrolling the park by dog team.

Photos on interpretive signs along this trail provide some sense of how this cabin was used many years aro by early travelers and workers in the park. Visitors can see for themselves, through these photographs, how the landscape changes during the winter months.

Bridge

Savage River Loop Trail

Savage River Bar Trail →

Parking

Parking

Savage Rock Trail

Park Road

Savage River Bar Trail

Trailhead: Mile 15 on the Park Road, just beyond the Savage River bridge. Take the Savage Canyon Trail until the Savage River Bar Trail turns off of it on the right. The Bar Trail loops back around to the Savage Canyon Trail 100 feet further on.

Distance/Time: 0.4 miles/0.6 kilometers one way, 30 minutes round trip.

Terrain: 60-inch-wide gravel trail along the edge of the Savage River, 25 foot/8 meter elevation change.

Difficulty: Easy, ADA accessible.

The wide gravel path heads toward the canyon, but diverts down to the large gravel bar on the river's edge. Mew gulls are ever present here during the summer, strutting around on the gravel bar. They feed on mice, voles, and insects. Visitors are strictly forbidden to feed the gulls because our food is not good for them.

Early in the season, visitors might be lucky enough to see rock ptarmigan, willow ptarmigan and white-tailed ptarmigan all together. They live in large mixed flocks during the winter and early spring, and then disperse in the summer.

All vegetation here is close to the ground—shrubs and other ground-hugging plants. All plants in the sub-arctic grow under harsh conditions. Winters last seven or eight months, the short growing season stretches to four months, and rainfall measures a scant 15 inches per year.

This wide gravel bar offers a first-hand look at how the river constantly changes. Upstream of the bridge, the Savage River is braided and river channels continually shift. In fact, the original Savage Bar Trail had to be rebuilt after the river reclaimed it. The wilderness is dynamic and ever changing at Denali National Park and Preserve.

Savage River Loop Trail

Trailhead: Mile 15 on the Park Road, just beyond the Savage River bridge.

Distance/Time: 1.6 miles/2.5 kilometers roundtrip, 1.5 hours.

Terrain: 24-inch-wide gravel path along edge of river between steep canyon walls, surface can be slippery if wet. 102 foot/31 meter elevation change.

Difficulty: Moderate.

Before you begin hiking this trail, take a careful look around. Imagine you are at the toe of a giant glacier. Thousands of years ago, that is exactly where you would be standing. To the south, a wide, rounded, U-shaped valley was formed by a giant glacier. Look downstream to the north, and the canyon is steep and narrow, formed by an ancient rushing river.

The trail leads directly into the steep canyon, down one shore, across a footbridge, and back on the other side. The trail starts out flat and wide and soon becomes a narrow gravel path that leads up and over some steep rock and gravel slopes.

Although quite popular and heavily used, this trail still provides plenty of wildlife sightings. Marmots and pikas make their homes on the hillsides among piles of rocks. It's not unusual to see Dall sheep, either up high on nearby ridges or even hopping across the river.

Birdwatchers may spot harlequin ducks. These colorful birds spend most of their lives at sea. They return every year to nest here near fast, clear, running water. It is not uncommon to see pairs of these ducks calmly bobbing down the churning rapids of the Savage River.

American dippers, America's only truly submersible songbird, also live along this river. Dippers dip up and down nearly forty times per minute while perched. They are totally dependent on the stream for their food, eating insect larvae, fish eggs, and flying insects.

With the rushing stream on one side and the tundra reaching into a mountain ridge on the other side of the trail, this is a wonderful wilderness excursion that can take one hour or half a day. It provides a sense of an even wider wilderness beyond Savage River.

Wildflowers

Wildflowers growing on the tundra in clumps of color may look small and dainty, but they are extremely hardy. These plants take root in rock crevices, and the barest of soils. The most common wildflowers include moss campion, white mountain avens, forget-me-nots, mountain harebells, and saxifrage. Surprisingly, few wildlfowers are red. That's because insects are the prime pollinators, and they are most attracted to yellows, blues, and whites. Wildflowers put all their energy into their blossoms; plant size doesn't matter on the sub-arctic tundra. They sprawl outward instead of upward, forming mats or mounds.

Savage Rock Trail

Trailhead: Mile 15 on Park Road at Savage River parking lot.

Distance/Time: 0.3 miles/0.5 kilometers one way, allow 30 minutes roundtrip.

Terrain: 30-inch-wide gravel trail with rock steps, steep, rocky, 128 foot/39 meter elevation change, grades up to 20 percent.

Difficulty: Moderately strenuous to strenuous.

Although not clearly visible from the parking lot, a carefully placed gravel trail leads up the south side of Savage Rock. Man-made steps make climbing easy and it doesn't take long before you climb high enough for sweeping views of surrounding countryside. Walking between the boulders on this trail makes you feel as if you are walking between the battlements of an ancient fortress. Part way up, a small grove of balsam poplar trees offers some shade.

Lichen are visible on many of the boulders. These plants are fragile and slow-growing. A lichen colony the size of a quarter may be ten years old. Lichens are easily crushed, particularly when dry or brittle. Admire them but don't step on them.

Behind Savage Rock, the trail ends with views of the Savage River as it roars down the steep canyon to the north. Be careful if climbing on Savage Rock itself. Loose rocks and boulders can make footing unsafe. There are many social trails in this area, but please resist straying off the established path, and causing further damage to plants.

Savage Rock is there because it has resisted weathering over the eons. In other parts of the Savage Canyon, look for signs of folded rock, caused by layers of rock subjected to intense pressure. That is characteristic of mountains in the "Outer Range." The rocks of the Outer Ranger are much older than the rocks of the Alaska Range that can be seen south, from atop Savage Rock.

Trails Past Savage River

Trails deep inside Denali National Park and Preserve may be reached by taking the visitor transportation system (VTS) bus shuttle. Let the VTS bus driver know where you want to get off the bus. You may catch a different bus returning to the entrance area any time during the day as long as there are seats available. During the busy season, in July, you may have to wait for a bus with empty seats.

Polychrome Trail

Trailhead: Take the VTS shuttle system to the Polychrome Rest Area at mile 46 on the Park Road.

Distance/Time: 0.5 miles/0.8 kilometers roundtrip, 15 minutes.

Terrain: 48-inch-wide trail with soil surface. One short, steep staircase and a steep section of trail lead to a flat plateau with an excellent view. 50 foot/15 meter elevation change.

Difficulty: Easy.

This loop trail can easily be experienced in its entirety during the short rest stop on the shuttle bus system. Get off the bus and walk up the stairs. The trail is located above and behind the rest area. From the top of the steps, a dirt path leads even higher. Nothing impedes the view in all directions once the roof of the shelter, the road, and buses are hidden from sight below.

The floor of the valley that comprises Polychrome Pass stretches to the mountains on the horizon. The peaks that mark the horizon are banded with yellow, orange, lavender and white rocks. These are volcanic rocks— basalt, andesite and rhyolite— which erupted onto the Earth's surface as magma and ash 40 to 60 million years ago. The colors vary in intensity as the light changes throughout the day.

For a closer look at wilderness, examine the ground along the sides of the trail. Wildflowers such as alpine forget-me-nots, moss campion, and mountain avens carpet the tundra, clinging tenaciously to life in a harsh environment. There are only about 150 species of wildflowers at Denali.

This dry tundra ecosystem is fragile and hikers walking off the trail can inadvertently cause damage to the plants that can take years to regenerate. Please enjoy the vegetation and views from the trail.

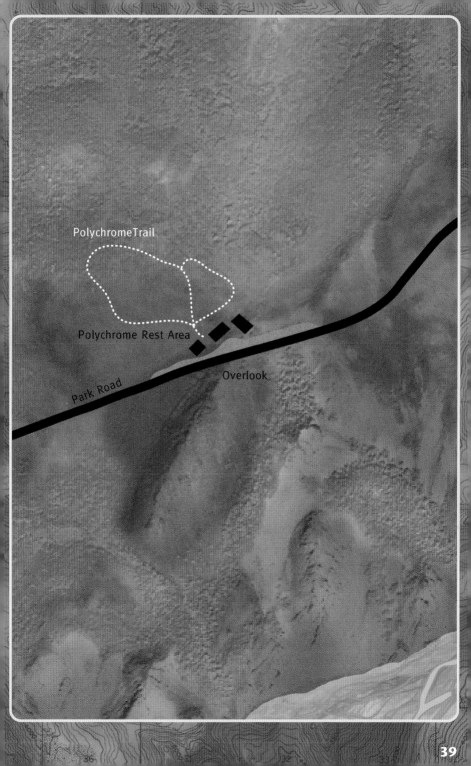

PolychromeTrail

Polychrome Rest Area

Overlook

Park Road

Alpine Ridge Trail

Trailhead: Take the VTS shuttle bus to Eielson Visitor Center at mile 66 on the Park Road. Look for the trailhead sign across the road from the visitor center.

Distance/Time: 2.2 miles/3.4 kilometers, about 2 hours roundtrip.

Terrain: 18-inch-wide trail of native soil. Very steep, with rock steps, sections of trail that are 25 percent grade and soils that are slippery when wet make this a difficult trail. 1000 foot/305 meter elevation change.

Difficulty: Strenuous.

Sixty-six miles into the park, the Alpine Ridge Trail provides an invigorating hike up into wild alpine country, directly across from Eielson Visitor Center. The trail follows a series of switchbacks. The trail is virtually invisible from the trailhead, which is found right across from the visitor center.

There are some long, gradual uphills before the trail gets steeper, continually climbing the entire way. Human-made steps make hiking a tad easier on some of the switchbacks. Wildflowers line the path, including moss campion, fireweed, shrubby cinquefoil, dryas, and goldenrod. Dryas grows in dry soil, usually along glacial streams or riverbeds. But it is also found here, on the windy slopes of Thorofare Mountain. Tundra is fragile here, so please stay on the trail.

It doesn't take long to get high enough to see to the other side of the river, where a kettle pond gleams on a tundra bench. The park road is visible both east and west. To the sides of the trail, scree slopes slide down the mountain. Among the jumbles of rock, look and listen for the diminutive pika. Even in mid- and late summer, patches of snow may hug some of the ravines that get little direct sunlight.

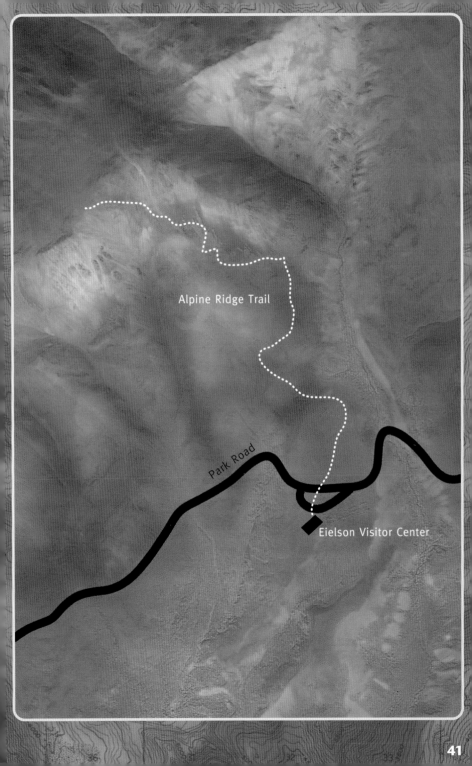

Alpine Ridge Trail

Park Road

Eielson Visitor Center

The top of the trail opens onto flat and wide-open space, offering views not only of Mount McKinley, but of terrain unseen from the Park Road. From here, hikers can take off in almost any direction and immerse themselves in the wilderness of Denali. Once you cross over the flat top of the trail, all traces of civilization melt away. Only wind, sky and mountains remain.

This is a stellar hike for spotting high alpine birds like surfbirds. These stout birds come to Denali to breed and eat insects on the alpine tundra. Other birds nest in the tundra too, including wheatears that fly here from Africa, and long-tailed jaegers, that nest at Denali and spend the rest of their lives at sea. There are four different kinds of falcons at Denali National Park, but gyrfalcons are the only falcons that spend the winter here. They are also the largest falcon in the world and the one most birders travel to Denali to see. Gyrfalcons sweep the slopes of Thorofare Mountain in search of ground squirrels and ptarmigan.

The saddle at the top of the trail may once have been the vent of an old volcano. Once you're on top, the alpine ridgeline stretches before you. You can seemingly walk forever.

Tundra Loop Trail

Trailhead: Take the VTS shuttle bus to Eielson Visitor Center at mile 66 on the Park Road.

Distance/Time: 0.4 miles/0.6 kilometers roundtrip; 0.2 miles/0.4 kilometers for Spur Trail, allow 30 minutes.

Terrain: 48-inch-wide gravel trail, 195 foot/64 meter elevation change including Spur Trail, 8 percent grade.

Difficulty: Easy to moderate. No obstacles to wheelchairs (such as stairs).

This short loop trail begins and ends at Eielson Visitor Center. It offers easy walking on a primarily flat, four-foot-wide gravel trail, giving visitors a perfect place to stretch legs before the return bus trip. Your walk is in the shadow of Mount McKinley, only 33 miles away. On a clear day, it might be hard to watch your step, because your focus will be on the mammoth mountain directly in front of you.

Wildflowers cover this tundra bench in spring and arctic ground squirrels regularly scurry back and forth across the tundra, stopping occasionally to stand at attention on hind legs. When you're at the far end of the loop, and Eielson Visitor Center is behind you, relish that feeling of nothing standing between you and the tallest mountain in North America. Feel the wind whoosh past your ear; see it bring in the wispy clouds that will soon hide Mount McKinley from view.

There are two spur trails that exit off the Tundra Loop Trail. The Tundra Spur is a short side trail that leads to the edge of the tundra bench, overlooking the valley below. The Gorge Creek Trail takes hikers down off the bench to the valley where Gorge Creek joins the Thorofare River. Both of these spur trails lead you just a bit further from buildings and buses and one step closer to wilderness.

Park Road

Eielson Visitor Center

Tundra Loop Trail

Tundra Spur Trail

Gorge Creek Trail

Blueberry Hill Trail

Trailhead: Take the VTS shuttle bus to the Wonder Lake Ranger Station or the north end of Wonder Lake. The trail connects the two points.

Distance/Time: 0.6 miles/1.0 kilometers roundtrip, allow 30 minutes.

Terrain: 24-inch-wide gravel and soil trail with some moderately steep sections, 111 foot/34 meter elevation change, grades up to 15 percent.

Difficulty: Easy to moderate.

There's a reason the trail up and around this knoll is called Blueberry Hill. In August and September, bushes laden with blueberries carpet this mound. On a clear day, hikers can munch on the sweet berries while admiring a full view of Mount McKinley.

The National Park Service developed this trail to urge hikers not to trample the tundra sedge mat in the Wonder Lake area. Nearby Wonder Lake provides a haven for birds and birders. It is home to grebes, pintails, other ducks, and a pair of nesting red-throated loons. The lake is 2.5 miles long, one-half mile wide and 280 feet deep. The outlet used to be at the south end of the lake, but now, it is located right across from the inlet, at the north end. The outlet is named Lake Creek and that water flows into Moose Creek. Inlet water comes from Ranger Pond, a small body of water with a beaver lodge built right in the middle, adjacent to the Wonder Lake Ranger Station. Look for this pond from the top of Blueberry Hill.

The trail begins at the base of the hill, near the north end of Wonder Lake, at the section of road built over the inlet. Strategically placed boardwalks allow easy access to the knoll. Feet stay dry and wet tundra remains untouched. The narrow

Park Road

Blueberry Trail

Wonder Lake
Ranger Station

Park Road

Wonder Lake

trail is only wide enough for one person at a time, so walk in single-file.

Low on the knoll, small, stunted spruce trees show obvious signs of the area's blasting winds. Their trunks and branches are rough and abraded. The trail winds through alder bushes and some small white spruce trees.

The trail eventually leads uphill to dry alpine tundra covered with bearberry plants, whose leathery, thumb-shaped leaves turn bright red in the fall.

Looking south, the first ridge in the distance is known locally as Ansel Adams Point. Local legend claims that the famous landscape photographer stood at that point to take his famously classic black-and-white photograph of Mount McKinley.

Miles beyond rest the two tallest mountains in the Alaska Range—Mount McKinley and Mount Foraker. They are flanked by other peaks that range as high as 13,000 feet.

At the top of the trail, look toward your feet. In places, the ground is covered with thin, flat, broken layers of gray-colored mica schist, which is a type of very old metamorphic rock. The trail continues south along the old glacial moraine, then back to the road.

McKinley Bar Trail

Trailhead: Mile 85.7 Park Road. South side of the road.

Distance/Time: 5 miles/8 kilometers roundtrip, allow 5 hours.

Terrain: 16- to 24-inch-wide dirt trail that is mostly flat with a few short slopes, 112 foot/34 meter elevation change.

Difficulty: Easy to moderate.

This is the route early sourdough climbers used to reach Mt. McKinley. Modern climbers use this same route today to approach the mountain from the north side, trudging up the Muldrow Glacier.

The trail begins near the top of the road that leads to Wonder Lake Campground, on the left side. One-person wide, the trail heads south through a mixture of open tundra, bog, and taiga forest. Blueberry bushes line early portions of the trail.

Spruce trees only chest-high may be thirty-five to forty years old. Age can be calculated by counting the number of new branches growing from the tree's trunk. In spots, clumps of black spruce called "dog-haired stands" cling stubbornly to life. Their moss-covered bottom limbs take root in the soil, looking like black tentacles reaching into the ground. It takes four years for a black spruce to develop a cone to spread its seed. White spruce produce cones annually.

Black spruce trees commonly grow in boggy areas. They are thin and scraggly, with shallow roots. Wildfire experts call them "gasoline on a stick." When wildfire strikes, black spruce trees become hot torches and flames can hop from treetop to treetop. Their needles are covered with a waxy substance that burns well. Black spruce cones, generally located atop the tree, require heat before they will open fully.

The trail turns from dirt to rock. Watch your step here. Look at the rocks carefully. Many have split

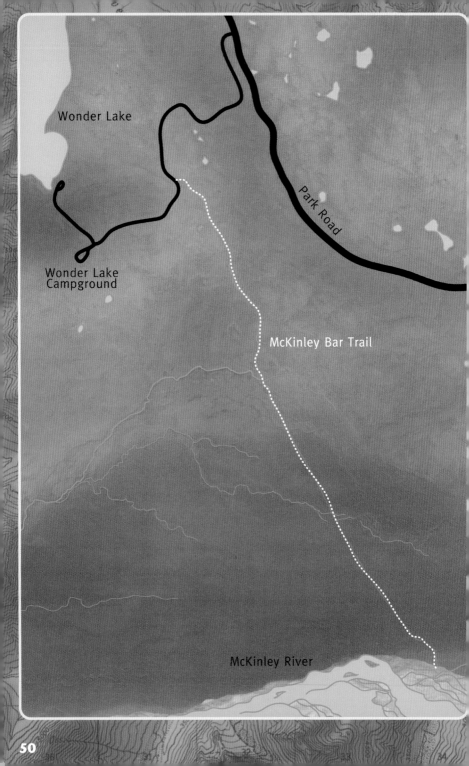

Wonder Lake

Wonder Lake
Campground

Park Road

McKinley Bar Trail

McKinley River

because water seeped into fissures in the rock, freezing and cracking the rock into pieces.

A side trail to a small knoll provides an overview of the valley below and a hint of where mountain climbers must hike to reach the base of Mount McKinley. Once arriving at the McKinley River, climbers must go further, enduring a long, spongy, wet tundra slog to Turtle Hill, a broad hump in the distance. From there, a short hike leads to Cache Creek and onto the Muldrow Glacier. Luckily, day hikers can enjoy a more casual outing and focus on closer vistas. Moose may be seen feeding in this area.

After the knoll, the path spills into giant meadows fed by natural springs. Look for sundews, carnivorous plants that eat bugs. Sundews look like tiny hands with many sticky fingers waving from the moss. The blobs of jelly on the ends of the "fingers" trap insects, which are digested by the plant. They thrive in wet soil.

Boardwalks cross these boggy areas now, eliminating the many spiderlike "social trails" once made by hikers trying to find the driest route through the swamp. Look for wildflowers. After the swamp, the trail leads through taiga forest, alive with songs by thrushes and sparrows.

Dwarf dogwood grows on either side of the trail. The four white "petals" of the dogwood blossoms are called bracts, which are specialized leaves. The actual flowers are tiny and are in a cluster in the middle of the bracts. Every fall, these flowers become bright orange berries called bunchberries. These are inedible. In spring, the white flowers of dwarf dogwood are often mistaken for wild strawberry.

Directly ahead, down the trail and through the trees, a big, white mountain comes into view. Often mistaken for Mount McKinley, this is really Mount Mather, named for Stephen Mather, the first director of the National Park Service. Mather wholly endorsed Charles Sheldon's 1915 proposal to turn Mount McKinley into a wildlife preserve, which led two years later to the creation of Mount McKinley National Park.

As soon the first balsam poplar tree is visible, you know you have reached the edge of the McKinley River gravel bar. As you leave the forest behind, look closely for green orchids and dryas, which grow profusely in this area. Dryas always indicates dry soil and good camping.

Pay attention to where you exit the trail when you leave the forest. It can be difficult to find again once you wander onto the vast riverbed of the McKinley River.

The McKinley River gravel bar is huge and the river channels are always changing. Feel free to walk along the river bar. Sometimes you can hop across small tributaries. Many are too dangerous and high to cross. The sense of freedom and wildness can be exhilarating here, where Mount McKinley fills the horizon and the nearest convenience store is 80 miles away.

Safety

- Tell someone where you are going and when you plan to return.

- As you hike, be alert and make plenty of noise (sing, talk loudly, yell every few minutes) so you will not surprise moose or grizzly bears.

- If you encounter a grizzly bear, DO NOT RUN. Like all predators, grizzlies tend to chase things that run. If a bear senses your presence, help to identify yourself by waving your arms over your head, clapping your hands, and by talking in a deep voice. Then, back off slowly and choose another route. Playing dead is only recommended if physical contact is certain. For more detailed guidelines, read the article "Bears, Avoiding Close Encounters" in the park newspaper, the *Denali Alpenglow*.

- If you encounter a moose, do not approach it. Run if a moose charges. Moose are very protective of their immediate space and of their calves. As soon as you leave, the moose will most likely calm down.

- Be on the lookout for areas that are closed to all entry (critical wildlife habitat or hazardous areas) as well as for trail crews who are improving trails in order to minimize resource damage.

Suggessted Reading

Look for these titles at the Alaska Natural History Association bookstore adjacent to the Denali Visitor Center, or on the web at www.alaskanha.org

Safety and Trail Etiquette
Leave no Trace in Denali National Park & Preserve Video, National Park Service. Alaska Natural History Association, 29 minutes.

Backcountry Bear Basics, Dave Smith. 1997. The Mountaineers, 110 pp.

Birds
Birds of Denali: An Introduction to Selected Species, Carol McIntyre, Nan Eagleson, and Alan Seegert. Illustrations by David Allen Sibley. 2002. Alaska Natural History Association, 64 pp.

Bird Checklist of Denali National Park, Kenneth Kertell, Doug Murphy, Alan Seegert, and Carol McIntyre. 2006. Alaska Natural History Association.

Wildlife
Grizzlies of Mount McKinley, Adolph Murie. 1985. University of Washington Press and Alaska Natural History Association, 270 pp.

Mammals of Denali, Adolph Murie. 1962, 1994. Alaska Natural History Association, 80 pp.

Wolves of Mount McKinley, Adolph Murie. University of Washington Press and Alaska Natural History Association, 260 pp.

Wildlife Guide: Denali National Park and Preserve, Kris Capps, 1994. Companion Press, 36 pp.

Geology
The Geology of Denali National Park and Preserve, Michael Collier. 1997. Alaska Natural History Association, 48 pp.

Sculpted by Ice: Glaciers and the Alaska Landscape, Michael Collier. 2004. Alaska Natural History Association, 122 pp.

Plants
Wildflowers of Denali National Park and Interior, Verna Pratt. Alaskakrafts, 166 pp.

Tanaina Plantlore, Priscilla Russell Kari. 1995. Alaska Native Language Center, Alaska Natural History Association & National Park Service, 224 pp.

History
Denali: Symbol of the Alaskan Wild, William E. Brown. 1993. Alaska Natural History Association, 224 pp